PERLA COLLECTION

ISBN 978-1-911424-96-3
SKU/ID 9781911424963

Cover design by Fabio Perla
"LA MADONNA DEI SOGNI"
Monochrome Pencils on wood - size cm70 x 80 - Year 2006

Book design by Wolf Graham
Editor: Wolf Graham

Publishing Company:
Black Wolf Edition & Publishing Ltd.
Scotland
www.blackwolfedition.com

Copyright © 2016 by Black Wolf Edition & Publishing Ltd.

All rights reserved. - First Edition: 2016

Name _____
Surname _____
Address _____
_____
Phone _____
Mobile _____
E-mail _____

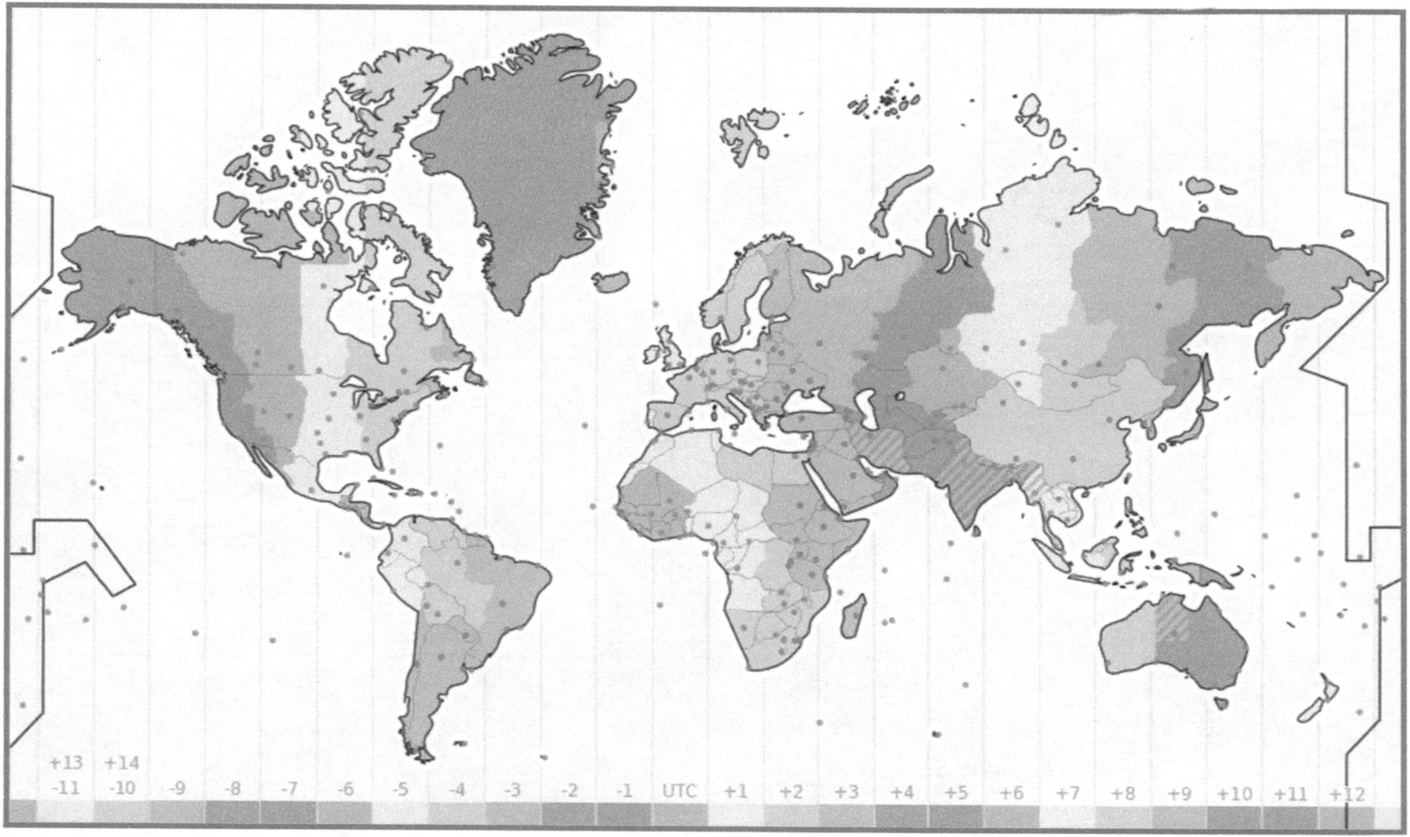
+13
+14
-11
-10
-9
-8
-7
-6
-5
-4
-3
-2
-1
UTC
+1
+2
+3
+4
+5
+6
+7
+8
+9
+10
+11
+12

PERLA COLLECTION

SKETCHES

ISBN 978-1-911424-96-3
SKU/ID 9781911424963

Cover design by Fabio Perla
"LA MADONNA DEI SOGNI"
Monochrome Pencils on wood - size cm70 x 80 - Year 2006

Book design by Wolf
Editor: Wolf

Publishing Company:
Black Wolf Edition & Publishing Ltd.
2 Glebe Place, Burntisland KY3 0ES, Scotland
www.blackwolfedition.com

Copyright © 2016 by Black Wolf Edition & Publishing Ltd.
All rights reserved. - First Edition: 2016

www.ingramcontent.com/pod-product-compliance
Lightning Source LLC
Chambersburg PA
CBHW031103080526
44587CB00011B/810